Under an Adirondack Moon

O. Bashaw, 1952

Under an Adirondack Moon

Poems

C. Ann Kodra

Iris Press
Oak Ridge, Tennessee

Cover Photo: Moon Over the AuSable River, Allison Arnold (2016)

Book Design: Robert B. Cumming, Jr.

Library of Congress Cataloging-in-Publication Data

Names: Kodra, C. Ann, 1954- author.
Title: Under an Adirondack moon : poems / C. Ann Kodra.
Description: Oak Ridge, Tennessee : Iris Press, [2017] | Includes
  bibliographical references.
Identifiers: LCCN 2017026826 | ISBN 9781604542424 (softcover : acid-free
  paper)
Classification: LCC PS3611.O3617 A6 2017 | DDC 811/.6—dc23
LC record available at https://lccn.loc.gov/2017026826

Acknowledgments

With thanks to the following journals and anthologies where these poems first appeared, sometimes in earlier versions:

Blueline: "Carrying Water"
Cutthroat (online): "Intussusception"
drafthorse: "Richard Benedict's Clock"; "Sweet Sin, 1939"; "The Ghosts of Horses Who knew Him"
Familiar Landscapes: "Hard Winter"; "Lining Bees"; "Homemade Coffin"
Memoir Journal: "Red Corn"; "Sarah Joy"
MOTIF (Vol. 3): "A Prison Guard's Confession to His Daughter"
New Millennium Writings: "The Shovel"; "Walking to the Outhouse in Winter"
Peacock Journal: "What I Remember Is One Thing"; "When I Tell Her of My Impending Divorce"
RHINO: "Dowsing"
Saranac Review: "His Last Dog"; "Still Life, with Longing"
The New Writer: "The AuSable"

With heartfelt gratitude to the following people who have appeared on my writing path and enhanced the journey exponentially:

Bob Cumming and Beto Cumming of Iris Press, for a smooth and gracious book journey.

Marilyn Kallet, Rita Sims Quillen, and Don Williams, for reading the manuscript and offering generous words of praise for the back of this book.

Austin Kodra, special appreciation for reviewing this entire manuscript multiple times and offering priceless corrections, suggestions, and encouragement.

My Knoxville women's writing group (MaryAnn Donaldson, Jamie Elliott Keith, Lucy Sieger, and Jenny Weisent), goddesses all, for being the best writing friends and fans a poet could have, and for reading and improving so many of these poems; special appreciation to Jamie Elliott Keith, who offered much additional help, encouragement, and a sharp eye and ear throughout the revision and proof stages.

The Advanced Poetry Group of the Knoxville Writers' Guild (Bob Cumming, Beto Cumming, Judith Duvall, Jamie Elliott Keith, Dale Mackey, John C. Mannone, and Rebecca Warren), for excellent poetry sharing, sage guidance during the formation of this collection, and sincere encouragement from the start; special appreciation to Bob Cumming, who teaches me so much of what I know about poetry.

My Muses: Linda Parsons and Jane Sasser, for eager ears, wonderful poems, and writing wisdom; special thanks to Linda Parsons, who traveled the distance with this book by offering early, middle, and final wisdom, encouragement, and expert editorial input.

So many other writers who have influenced me with their words and kindness—too many to name here, and finally ...

My family (Ron Kodra, Evan Kodra, Austin Kodra, and Korey Shields), for being incredibly supportive and eternally loving.

To my father,
who gave me the gift
of naming trees, plants, animals, mountains, and streams

To Ron,
my husband and best friend,
who says, "Write!" and means it—
my heart belongs to you

Contents

Loving Mountains More • 15

I. Crow Moon

The Allen Place • 19
Slap Her Hard • 21
Sarah Joy • 22
Sweet Sin, 1939 • 23
Richard Benedict's Clock • 25
Unexpected Shepherd • 26
Make-Believe Straws • 27
Nellie and Frank • 28
Lining Bees • 30
Hard Winter • 33
Dowsing • 35
Carrying Water • 37
Changes • 38

II. Strawberry Moon

The AuSable • 43
Woodchuck Beans • 44
Horsepower • 45
Blind Stud • 46
Work Loved Well • 48
The Tindale Place, 1944 • 49
A Hawk, a Dove, a River of Sound • 51
The Telling • 52
Nothing Accidental in the Felling of a Tree • 54
Red Corn • 55

III. Hunter's Moon

Like Horses • 59

What I Mean When I Say *Amen* • 60

Walking to the Outhouse in Winter • 61

Caged Bird • 62

Adirondack Girl • 63

A Prison Guard's Confessions to His Daughter • 65

When I Tell Her of My Impending Divorce • 66

Intussusception • 67

My Grandmother in the Hospital for the Last Time • 68

My Father's Father, Undone • 69

The Silence of Missing • 71

The Shovel • 73

Epitaph for His Draft Horses • 74

Homemade Coffin • 75

IV. Snow Moon

Adirondack Moon • 79

How to Swallow • 80

Drifting from This World • 82

Still Life, with Longing • 83

Canon, Room 346 • 85

What I Remember Is One Thing • 86

My Father's Last Night • 87

His Last Dog • 88

My Father Has Traveled On • 89

Dear Earth • 90

How I Remember Him • 92

Afterword

The Ghosts of Horses Who Knew Him • 95

The Bashaw Family • 97

Notes • 99

Author's Note

When Oril Vernon Bashaw was almost two years old, his father carried him home one clear night from his paternal grandparents' house. Looking up at the uncountable stars, the man who would become my father pointed and said, "See the moon, lookum lots!" Years later, near the end of his life in the Adirondack Mountains of New York State, my father said he had seen the moon, the stars, and much more, and that he had lived a mostly good and satisfying life.

On my father's request in 1997, I typed his handwritten memoir over the course of a few months. I noticed several things in the process. He wrote well for a farmer's son with only a high school education, one at times spotty because of more pressing farm duties. He made few errors in the family history, and those he did make were corrected before the manuscript went to print.

And finally, it felt odd to me that he didn't include much about his marriage or children. Those omissions even stung a little, but ultimately they made sense in view of his chosen audience: his children. My two brothers and I would know our early histories through the personal lenses of our lives and family storytelling.

In his never-published memoir, my father said of his childhood and adolescence: "I did not ever feel deprived in any way." He went on to note that although there were material things he wished for, not receiving them all never mattered much to him. He had two sisters, a dog, and eventually a horse and a hunting rifle. He counted these as inestimable treasures, along with "an unbridled imagination."

Although my father and I had a difficult relationship throughout my youth, it smoothed out some as we both grew older and wiser. We took much pleasure in sharing the things we loved: books, nature, horses, dogs, gardening, and cooking. I wrote many poems about my father over the past five or six years, and one day it occurred to me that I was not only drawing material from his memoir, but I was also teaching myself, through carefully mined lines of poetry, who he had been as a child, teenager, and young man. The geography and climate of the rural area he grew up in, as well as the influence of family and extended family, helped shape him for better and for worse, as such factors shape us all. He could no more be separated from the mountains and streams and people he loved than from his own skin.

As I read and reread my father's memoir, all the while crafting additional poems about his life, the idea of a larger tribute was born—one that would develop into a reflection and interpretation of his life. This retelling in poetry springs from the solid foundation of his apt storytelling, his engaging memoir, and my memories of him in his middle and later years. *Under an Adirondack Moon* is a labor of love and a desire to better understand my father. I have tried to stay true to his life within its pages. I hope these poems will offer readers a unique and satisfying journey through the life of an Adirondack man.

—C. Ann Kodra

I hurried with him to our orchard-plot,
And he beheld the moon, and, hushed at once,
Suspends his sobs, and laughs most silently,
While his fair eyes, that swam with undropped tears,
Did glitter in the yellow moon-beam! Well!—
It is a father's tale: But if that Heaven
Should give me life, his childhood shall grow up
Familiar with these songs, that with the night
He may associate joy.

—Samuel Coleridge (from "The Nightingale")

Loving Mountains More

for the Adirondack Mountains

Stay longer than a breath, for the mountain
inhales deeper than grass or sand or even bodies
    of water. Under the craggy face hulks a lung,
a bellows drawing cool, earthy air, exhaling
    the damp, quivering heart of stone. Lose yourself
in billowing breaths swooping through
    cave-hardened space. The fierce edge of life
bleeds out through mineral veins, glaciates
    cells one by one, stalactites echoing the slow syllables
of your new voice pooling
    in the mirror beneath your feet.

I.

Crow Moon

The Allen Place

—1929, Trout Pond, NY

I never enjoyed running water, indoor plumbing,
or electricity until the age of eighteen … what
you never had, you never miss.
    —O. Bashaw

My earliest memory is an orchard,
my father wrote. He is not here to say,
in his smoke-graveled voice, that only a handful

of trees, huddled behind the clapboard house
where he was born, conspired to offer apples
to the family. At two-and-a-half years old,

he listened for a sister, Carol, delivered from
the dark world of before-ness to the dappled light
of farmhouse. From the back bedroom

the foreign warning wailed. Later the midwife
held my father firmly before the yellow warmth
of the kitchen woodstove, plunging

his wriggling body into the washtub while flames
leaned toward the open cast-iron doors and witnessed
a toddler demand the circle of his mother's arms.

Bath water, hauled early from the brook
down yonder, heated atop the same, oak-laden
stove, poured into the tub—same water that washed

dishes and soaked overalls, quenched the thirst
of horses and cows, cooled the dry, rural throats
of his mother and father—now

baptized my father into a shifting world,
streaming over hair and ears and shoulders
as he strained to hear the new sound again.

He was promised a fresh red apple, sliced
to fit stubby fingers, the juice to wander along
his dimpled wrist like a sweet autumn creek.

From cooling suds, he emerged an older brother,
stopped pleading so much for his mother. Stopped
missing what he once had but would barely remember.

Slap Her Hard

My father, born on the solid backs of stubborn
Bashaw men, said, *Slap her hard, just once
Grandma*, when at age three he didn't

get his way. Meaning, *Brand my mother's flesh
with your hand.* This story told over and over,
a wink and a chuckle at such a manly boy.

A lineage of years and wars and sturdy
women who wanted a husband, children,
a cow or two, and no bruises to mottle

plump country cheeks. Those steel-core
men marched back to Moses, my father's
father's grandfather, landholder who fought

Union-side in the 118th Adirondack Regiment,
Company C. Three years gone, Moses moved
from New York's Wilmington and Jay to the final

battle in Richmond, dodging red bullets and
Confederate prison. Once home, Moses turned a dandy,
drank moonshine till he wasn't sure he'd ever served.

His wife hid the vanilla extract behind her disappointment:
here, her man. This, her stinging slap from life
despite the maiden name of Joy.

Moses Bashaw
1843-1907
Served in the Civil War

Sarah Joy

—Gibson Hill, AuSable Forks, NY

My clearest memory of Grandma Sarah
is when she stopped at her house with my father
and me and served us applesauce cake.
                                                    —O. Bashaw

Sarah rose one morning, seventy-eight years
shaping her gait, and said to her son Frank,
I feel ill. My father's great-uncle eyed

his mother's poor color and replied, *Don't go
today, Ma. I'll pay you the dollar
you would have earned cleaning.*

A welcome vision of brooms and mops
and bed sheets flapped before Sarah's steady eyes;
she answered her son with love and long thought,

No, I'll go. It's the work I need, not the dollar.
Ten miles, round trip, she walked to complete
the day that needed completing, both legs

of the journey and everything in between
bringing a satisfaction that couldn't be
bought or sold or bargained.

Sweet Sin, 1939

My father ate forbidden cake in the open house
of the Lord. The annual offering of food borne
by children, made by mothers and grandmothers,

lifted high with pride as they hiked Trout Pond's shore
on a Sunday, settling gifts on wooden tables the fathers
set up beside water. The silenced clop of horses' hooves

and creaks of carts served as grace, and all bowed
their heads to plates. Main fare taken in, my father
crept close to the white-iced, two-tiered tower of sin,

a dessert rumored tainted by the sour dirt of disregard,
a cook unclean, unworthy of providing manna.
Murmurs of smells, cats on the table, shame:

this family whose mother baked a cake for her son
to bear on this day of rest, a batter blended with care
and expectant hope that every proffered communion

holds. Others passed it by. My father, hungry but shy,
nabbed a slice and ate it fast, then grabbed another.
Years later, he'd yet to suffer ill effects except remarks

of those better than a family who owned only an ox,
reason for gossip after church. The creature, harnessed
like a horse but for the heavy collar in reverse,

slow but powerful, plowed and ferried all their needs,
steady as a quicker steed. The beast hauled them into
a shaky tomorrow of crossed ocean and war that would soon

encroach on their humble stores, where cakes boasted
no sugar inside, the outsides bereft of a sweetened glaze.
Where the shunned family traded the ox for one old horse

and found their status raised—near level with neighbors;
no one stocked enough rationed staples to say her cakes
were sweeter, no one with a leftover crumb for a picnic lunch.

Richard Benedict's Clock

He did all his work with horses,
plowed and planted, harvested and rested.
The invention of the engine would ruin
the world, he told my father, a boy
who imagined a tangle of gears and switches
rising up, wielding oil-slick swords, slaying
children and parents at each farmhouse
nesting in the meadows.

By team and wagon or team and sleigh,
my father's grandfather drove the family
to visit a brother five miles away or took
Marthy to teach at the one-room school
when snow drifted too deep for boots.
*Grandpa Rich wore a shoulder yoke to carry
two pails of water, twelve quarts each,
from the spring.* A rope on each end of the yoke,
a hook for the bails, and my father ached
for the day when he could bear this load.

Richard Benedict, a horse-drawn man, refused
to change his clock to daylight savings time
in spring; neighbors lived an hour ahead of him.
My father's Aunt June would ask, *Are we coming
to supper by our time or yours?* But his horses
knew time, and he wagered their eager whinnies
to announce a dawn and dusk always arriving
just ahead of hunger, the steady clock
that marks a working man's life.

Unexpected Shepherd

> I decided to hide it up my nose.
> —O. Bashaw

When I was a child, I thought
    my grandfather might be quite
dangerous. Six feet five, he hulked
    over me—a giant in my world.
But my father told him a different way:
    an affectionate man who
fumbled with a thin, sharp wire.
    His trembling hands shaped
a miniature shepherd's hook,
    worked it into the left nostril
beside and behind the wedged,
    trespassing peanut whose salt already
burned the little boy's tender
    membranes, releasing a sting
of tears. *Easy now, don't move*
    an inch; I'll get the little devil out,
my grandfather might have said.
    His son recalled scant pain or fear,
just bulky hands plying the cobbled hook
    with gentle skill. The peanut, sent
promptly to the trash, set off a lecture
    on stashing small objects inside
any body orifice, even
    to win a family contest.

Make-Believe Straws

My mother sometimes
made root beer from
yeast, sugar-water,
and extract.
—O. Bashaw

Scallions snipped
fresh and pungent
from the garden,
their tops ready-
made cylinders.
He waited with
two siblings for
the buried white
circumference
to expand until
the green stood
sturdy, and then,
plunged into water
or soda, straws
were born.
Liquids sucked
up through
saporous cells
took on their
trademark taste:
water fresher
for the journey,
root beer sweeter
for the contrast.
(From time to time,
a bottle exploded,
cap too tight
for fermentation:
a different kind
of childhood fun.)

Nellie and Frank

Before I was born, my grandfather worked as a river-driver, floating logs
and pulp down the AuSable River to J.J. Rogers' mills.

—O. Bashaw

Frank took odd jobs—steady work soured his heart.
Known for skill with a double-bit axe, he cut
and charged by the cord, thinning out Taylor's Pond
and Black Brook's woods, tree by tree. He lined bees
and fished trout and threw a regulation
baseball hard and fast, cracked a one-inch pine board

propped on a split-rail fence, ruing the day
he turned down a chance to pitch for the pros
where trying out and training offered no pay.
He peered ahead to heavy hours thick with debt
and drifted back to the creek-lined world he knew.

Nellie made sweet butter from the Jersey cow's
cream. She beat it and beat it by hand with
a wooden spoon. Frank came home after work
or fishing to a table laden with butter
and homemade bread *renowned throughout
the county to rival illicit sex.*

*Made the best-tasting food on a shoestring
I've ever known.* Nellie grew pansies
and sunchokes, gathered wild asparagus
in spring, strawberries in late July.
She stirred oyster stew on Christmas, that one

decadent day. Every tooth pulled by age thirty-two,
Nellie never wore dentures, but those tough gums
could wrest a chunk from an autumn Macintosh,
skin and all. She wore a man's shoes, wrapped
her legs, compressing bad veins and girlish

dreams. My father rocked on the front porch while
his grandfather played harmonica late
into summer's star-drenched nights, long mournful
chords bearing them deep toward the beckoning
house of the Lord—valleys and mountains hallowed
by sun and shadow, by trembling, soulful praise.

Lining Bees

for Frank Bashaw, as told by his grandson

In the morning
my grandfather
rose early, urging
the fire to life
with women clad
only in bras
and panties,
scanty for
that time:
a page from
the Sears catalog
burned off
the predawn chill
along with his guilt.
After fried perch
and homemade bread,
he'd head outside
with a bee in a box
captured the day before,
now drunk
on a spent wedge
of honeycomb dredged
in sugar water
and oil of anise.
The bee, released,
would fly in concentric
circles high enough
to gain what sky it took
to strike out in a line
for its hive
in a hollow tree,
and then, being a bee,

deposited sweet nectar
in an empty comb,
winging its way
back to the box
for more.
While it stayed busy,
as bees are wont to be,
my grandfather
dabbed its derriere—
a tiny spot of white
paint borne
by a wooden match.
When the marked
bee once more
returned to air,
its flight could
be timed to see
how long the line
to the hive would be.
All morning I watched:
the sun rose, our shadows
shortened, the line
was timed. Back and forth,
shorter and shorter until
we both stood
still, listening
to the sound of buzzing
bees and gazing around
for hollow trees.
On a good day,
seventy to eighty pounds
of honeycomb could
be found in one
felled tree and heated
in pots on my grandfather's
old woodstove

to drain the liquid
gold from combs
and spread it, thick
and sweet, on buckwheat
cakes. The old man sat
beside me on the wooden
bench, honey dripping
from his lips, days
of lining bees swarming
to the corners
of his warm smile.

Hard Winter

—Trout Pond, NY

> One winter in the '30s, the temperature
> fell to 46 below zero. Most of our
> canned goods in the cellar froze.
> —O. Bashaw

My grandmother stepped carefully down
the steep, hand-cut stairs, no freezers
or refrigerators, nothing to miss

that she'd never known. Her hard work met
at the bottom, glint of broken glass and bits
of glistening green, red, and yellow strewn

across the firm-packed dirt. No one would go
hungry that winter, but the smorgasbord
of tomatoes, pickles, beans, and squash—gone.

My grandfather hunted harder for deer
and partridge, axed a hole in an iced Trout Pond,
dropped his line and hauled home smelt

in a sweet-grass creel. Few meaty hens made
it through to spring. Even the cocky rooster
toppled into a stew, old carcass boiled soft

to slippery bones in his own broth, marrow
sucked clean by each child's eager, shining lips
while barnyard cats hissed over the gizzard.

When spring finally sidled in, late May,
my grandmother huddled over hatchlings like
a fierce hen, groomed a male to become

head rooster, hoping the next winter would
not require his tough flesh in the stewing pot
slung ready over the wood-burning stove.

Dowsing

My father's father knew
how to dream water, how
to cant the forked stick,
witness its tilt over
earth stitched with cool,
coursing veins. Arm of his
art, the branch would twitch.
Roy's the man you want
for dowsing, other men
would say. A man who
couldn't recite the alphabet
or save a dollar to save
his farm, but knew something
others didn't, held a secret
even his deepest thoughts
couldn't sound. Was the magic
in the stick, the hand that tipped
it, or the thirsty heart roaming
the fields, ever seeking
a drink of pure conviction?
A dug well offered proof,
a mountain man's redemption,
so he wielded shovel too,
like a needle angled to mine
subterranean blood.
And when at the bottom
he finally tapped the lode
divining rod and fey
DNA had rooted out, when
the last gouge of metal scoop
loosed a gush of muddy water,
he clambered up, swinging
his body side to side, hands
on rope, boots pressed against

dirt walls crafted only hours
before, heaved the shovel
overhead with bellowed
warning, hoisted himself
toward the vast lip of land,
the swell of voices, the long
draught of worth his parched
brain had sought, the other
men—faces lit by sun—bending
beside the new well, warbling
chorus of liquid sap
rushing into its new, steep
stem, rising, deepening
even as they offered hands
to pull him onto higher ground.

Carrying Water

> ... because the fields were ours,
>> And by the brook our woods were there.
>
> We ran as if to meet the moon ...
>> —Robert Frost, "Going for Water"

My father's great-great-uncle, William Joy,
laid claim to an eight-inch arm that dangled loose
from the shoulder holding firm a decade past:
a mining mishap, iron ore, not gold,
but shining dust a northern pickaxe probed.
He hung a pail of water on the stump
extended straight, the bail slung over bone
and battered skin, a remnant of his trade.

Hair curly and gray, lips a bow of fun,
he bade his nephew call him Old Black Bill.
My father's mother cared for none of this,
nonsense to the core, she said, but still
her boy assessed it clever to own less
than half an arm and carry water thus
a quarter mile from brook to house. The stub
as red and cheerful as the uncle's face:
he bore this earthly burden much like joy.

Changes

When I was in the 4th grade,
we moved to the town of Lewis.
—O. Bashaw

My father's first taste of mean
arrived in a two-room school,
upscale: two teachers, not one.
Two big boys forced him into
the woodshed out back and piled
the doorway high with broad sticks
of oak and gnarled elm jammed tight
enough to imprison.

A game of Fox & Geese drowned out
his shouts for help until the teacher's
bell pronounced the end of fun.
She heard him then and scolded
the school bullies back outdoors
to free the blockade they'd stacked.

Another time they plunked him
on a swing, pushed him higher,
higher, two bullies twisting
metal chains so the swing spun
in cruel, dizzying arcs that turned
my father's face pale and sick
till they pushed him off for fear
of a punishing branch.

In high school, the gym teacher
and a crowd of laughing boys
shamed him farther up
the climbing ropes until his stomach
knotted with the treachery of height.
Gravity held the smug boys
below, safe from vertigo and
the bane of loft, those queasy evils
that lodged within my father forever.

He fled to his first adult job—
lumberjack, sawing and hurling
burly chunks of wood, a grounded
pile to bury all those bullies
over and over. Later he changed
his course once more to work
a high prison wall and walk
the narrow concrete.
In ghastly nighttime dreams
framed by intermittent rails,
he plunged that thirty feet
again and again, nearly killing
the last scrap
of spinning child within.

II.

Strawberry Moon

The AuSable

Every winter this river stole
blocks of my grandparents' land, claimed
the jagged terrain, mountains riven by a rough
strand of pools and rapids, wet rocks slicked
black by the slap of cold sky, ice fencing off
mammoth water rooms, delivering shape
to a shapeless ruler. Sections of creaking floes
broke into behemoths, heaved themselves like
prehistoric mammals onto land, carved out
earth to suit a peculiar greed, cracked the asphalt
seams of Route 9N, scraped the fields' shoulders,
stole pasture, and waited patiently for longer
sun-spanned hours, for return to the mother
river, to melt easily into beckoning
banks, trickle down to a stony bed.
River of Sand, changeling.

Woodchuck Beans

Oh, how we longed to fish away our Saturday.
An older Grandpa Frank told this story to my father
as they fished a brook cached in northern woods, lady's slippers
and trillium spattering the forest floor, dollops of pink and white
spilled light. Brown trout were biting; the day was calling.

Moses told his boys—Frank and Rollie—they could go after
they planted a heaping pail of white navy beans, inched them
into wavy, boy-scribed rows, a new crop of soup
for their mother's late-summer pot. Instead, the boys waited
till Moses wandered off to his stash in the hayloft,

a fine private perch where he'd nip from a jug while sons
reeled out a lazy afternoon's work. They promptly cast
those seeds down a creature-dug hole the convenient size
of a bucket of beans, then stomped false rows in the garden
plot with plain shoes that would soon carry them creek-side,

crude fishing rods arching toward sky. Moses wouldn't know till
a few weeks passed, surprised by spindly stems, choked growth
from a woodchuck hole—leaves, tiny blossoms nodding assent
to the clever boys' fun, fish long ago caught and fried. Moses
scolded them both: *Plant new rows!* If only the season would hold.

Horsepower

> When I was small, sometimes he would let me hold
> the reins and drive the team on a straight stretch of road.
>> —O. Bashaw

Grandpa Rich ran the farm with Billy and Jim
—bay geldings that did his bidding,
huffing sweet-clover breath
at the hand that stroked suede nose
and broad, bony forehead. In winter,
Richard Benedict hauled water into the house,
warmed it on the woodstove for the horses
to drink. At night, he laid clean straw for their beds.
Harnesses, oiled and rubbed supple,
hung on hooks in the horse barn,
a meticulous order only
he understood.

In the wagon shed: team sleds
and cutters, one-seat, two-seat,
and four-seat buggies, and one fine
fringed surrey. Sundays he hitched up
Billy and Jim, drove them two or three miles
for the trot they needed, for the fresh scene
that scratched his itch.

My father's grandfather worked the soil
with horse power: plowing, planting, reaping.
*He said the engine would ruin the whole damned
world.* The horses strained—sweat-sheened shoulders,
sinewy legs braced—never knowing their strength,
never guessing their terrible limits. Waiting
in the barn at the same time each day, they
bobbed their heads and swished their tails
for a pitchfork of fragrant hay and sometimes
a sweet apple.

Blind Stud

> This is a horse that has been castrated
> but still has the urge to mate with a mare.
> —O. Bashaw

My grandfather led the family to trust they'd stay.
Bought the house and land—the Brown Place in Trout Pond
—brief reprieve before my father's sophomore year.

They built a deck on the roof, shored up the front porch,
framed a cow barn, hammered up a four-stall garage
with space above for the hired men Roy believed

would come. Purchased his first sawmill in a line
of mills to plane hours into golden grains of practiced
ruin, shavings born of the hum

of portable mills shaping a feckless, portable
life. But the size of things planted budding hope
in my steadfast grandmother's freshly turned

heart, while the yard outside rustled and clattered
with chickens, sheep, and pigs, and cows she'd argued
long and hard to own. My grandfather, favoring horses,

lumber, and guns, gave in to the bovine herd:
a barbed-wire fence to raze the sense of being a man,
but his happy wife lay looser on her back at night.

Weekends and summers, their only son fed, watered,
and milked the livestock, gardened for the homestead, leaving
the men to spend their sweat on hay. Later my father labored

the forests with them, sawing logs and pulp with
crosscut, buck, and bow, single- and double-bit
axe; no chainsaw till '44 when they moved again,

five miles away to the Tindale Place in Clintonville.
My father's father blind to the way to hold onto
a farm. Sweat and soil cast behind, an angry nod

to neighbor men——resolve for that world slid away like
peeled bark, losing grip in daylight, harnessing newer,
riskier dreams under moonlight. Omen of things to come.

Work Loved Well

for Toby, who carries on the love of horses

Sergeant, Colonel, George, and Nell
ferried my father through the time
of skidding logs in work loved well.

The acrid scent of sawed white pine
and red oak floated up with neighs,
ferrying him through a stand of time:

eight hours each for years of days
the horses pulled their weight for him,
and red oak loaded up with neighs.

Fourteen hundred pounds in skin
as velvet as a lover's touch.
The horses pulled such weight for him:

one hundred and fifty pounds not much
to counter Clydesdale blood and might
as gentle as a lover's touch.

He learned to trust their sense and sight,
to guide them with a quiet word
that settled Clydesdale blood and might.

A really good horse, my father said
(Sergeant, Colonel, George, or Nell),
is guided with a quiet word
to skid the logs in work loved well.

The Tindale Place, 1944

> At the time we moved again, I turned 18. It was the nicest
> house we ever had.
>
> —O. Bashaw

The farmhouse my grandparents lived in loomed
and rambled, steep-pitched roof a shingled
hat for sunlit rooms: long pine tables, horsehair chairs,
here and there sepia ancestors bound in oak.

The house held Tindales first, miners come to ply
their picks into the land's crust, prying for the pith
of steel. Iron ore asleep couldn't dream its hard
new fate in a flyspeck town fast swollen
to thirty thousand, now shrunken and a mile from home.

Three hundred acres of Roy Bashaw's land flanked
the roiling AuSable River, monstrous blocks of ice
thrown high each early spring, flash thaws topping
its heaving banks. Each year the river stole a chunk

of my grandfather's farm. The thirty-stanchion
cow barn with six horse stalls stood its ground, along
with a five-bedroom house whose veins ran hot
and cold with plumbing, *two* bathrooms, kitchen,

dining room, living room, den, a large front stairway
leading to the hide-and-seek haven above, and
the secret escape: back stairs plunging to a closet hidden
behind the kitchen. In the cellar, a wood furnace

crouched like an ogre waiting to sling sparks
at unsuspecting boys. Twenty-five milking cows,
pigs and chickens, and six months' farm deferment
lent my father the work and time to change

from farm boy to man. World War II marched past,
and at the end of his half-year reprieve, he drew
the shaky breath of time's resolution.
Logging, farming, and bulldozing stoked his days,

his nights banked with books at the farmhouse table.
Eighteen, and he finally knew the comfort of a home
he wouldn't leave anytime soon.
Electric lights. Running water. Bottomland.

A Hawk, a Dove, a River of Sound

Because my father marries
        too soon, he grows the skin of an oak
that has lived its life leaning over
        the river, swept along in sound but never
motion. Inside the rush of reflection,
        he suffers deafness.
He cannot discern when a new tone
        trickles in, reaching the hardwood
of his heart. Sometimes a hawk cries out
        and lights on his outstretched arm,
surveying the folding and churning
        over gray-skinned river stone,
or it rises to the ageless sky,
        swept on rafts of clouds
aimless in their troubled reflection
        on the deaf suffering below.
Because my father weds too soon,
        he leans toward a current he didn't choose,
ignoring the reckless call of rising sap,
        its dark moan rustling heartwood,
not hearing the rush of wings,
        the river, the creak of leaning, forgetting
to reflect on the cloudless sky above.
        Because there is an aimless rush
of water, a reckless hawk, gathering clouds
        crowning the oak—and there stands my mother
in a rustle of dove-gray silk, white pearls
        at her throat—she doesn't
have to utter a sound.

The Telling

After Robert Winner

Who's gonna throw down bets on a no-win fight,
who's gone and lost his head tonight?
—The Rough & Tumble,
"Dog in This Fight" from *Pieces and Pieces*

Some devil twists my father into a gambler,
a whiskey drinker, before I'm born, before
he slips a thin gold band on my mother's finger.

My grandfather tells me this when
I'm a young mother myself, no longer sold
on parents turning the key to make

a family hum. Somewhere in the days
my father almost forgot to live, another woman
carved out space on his lap, and glasses sat

on the slick barroom table beside a fistful of cards
already dealt. *He never told us that*, I say,
and the hard flint of something akin to buckshot

strikes a spark behind my grandfather's clouded
eyes. If I could shake my father's teeth and tongue
to truth, I might remember where we were

when lies were born. But weighted with outs,
we both go on pretending we're card sharks,
and I grow up not learning the requisite skills

for losing. I'd like my father to remember how
he was a young man with dark, wavy hair,
cigarette slung between his lips, thin paper

sticking like a second skin, eyes shifting just
an inch awry from flush. I'd like him to admit
that final poker game, the one where he pushed

in all his chips, turned over a pair of twos,
and won a lifetime of regret passed on
to his children, who believed he knew best

and then stopped believing. *Every Saturday night,
my grandfather says, your father drove too fast
to The Forks, drank hard and gambled.*

Till he met your mother. Their faces hopeful, a long
bluff behind white smiles where everything honest
had been all-in, but then they simply folded.

Nothing Accidental in the Felling of a Tree

A double-bit axe is an ode to labor,
the sharp bits teeth to cleave tough fiber,

the cheeks wedged deep to lever the wood,
the inclined plane—a livelihood.

~

The simple machine worked toe to heel
to fell what forested family soil.

My father, clean shaven, the axe with beard;
he stroked the throat and studied it hard,

then gripped the haft, never choked the axe;
he eyed the axe and it eyed him back

while shoulders and belly and head revoked
all human thought when he chopped through oak.

He swung the axe and swung it true
and never questioned the arc it knew.

Red Corn

This is red corn. It will hold the blessing of abundance … red corn
from the West that gives long life as our spirits travel westward
with the sun.

> —Native American belief

Back when I was a boy, he told me,
they had what was called a Corn Husker's Bee
for fodder corn, not sweet corn. See
the boys would flock to these gatherings
on the promise of a kiss from any girl
on the premises if a boy could husk
a red ear of corn.

How often did you find a red ear of corn?

Not often, he remembered. Then,
but often enough. The girls
who weren't willing didn't attend.
You could kiss any girl you wanted.

One kiss for one red ear of corn.

What makes it red?
He didn't know and said
he never asked.
But a lot of corn got husked.

One girl for one red ear of corn.

This as he perched at the sink
on his stool, stripping corn with
faltering hands, forearms blotched
by purple bruises, ears pale
but sweet with remembering.

III.

Hunter's Moon

Like Horses

After Wendell Berry

Suppose we lived our days
like horses, breathing, breathing—
completing our work with no restraint,

pulling the weight of hours
for the tart surprise of an apple,
stacking the sweet minutes without complaint?

What I Mean When I Say *Amen*

After Geffrey Davis

> Fathers, do not embitter your children,
> or they will become discouraged.
> —Colossians 3:21

The Sunday my father gave the sermon—after our minister
left for the weekend, after the church women begged
and my father said yes, writing long into Saturday night—

my mother cringed, my older brother snorted. I witnessed
with wide eyes, never hearing a word he read, but choking
on the fact that this man, who sat at our dinner table and stormed

at sins as small as a boy growing long hair—as though that
act alone would make or break him—could speak such measured words,
could sway the staunchly gathered Protestants. I watched his hands

shake when he turned pages thinned with oft-thumbed doubt,
though his voice remained steady, all-knowing. Later I learned
to talk back in that same solid voice, to sound my words in sureness

though my hands trembled, to snap syllables like clean pages in the wind,
suspended by the grip of before and after, times he snatched his rifle,
spun gravel from our driveway, and my mother, quaking with something

like change, threatened to replace the locks on her heart, to try another
combination to long, tumultuous hours. I learned to speak in angry
tongues, to tell the other truth of *home*, the kind to end in threats

or leaving. Not even God could stop me. No wonder we were all
so taken aback, no wonder we all held our breath as one when
my father looked right at us, bowed his head, and said *Amen*.

Walking to the Outhouse in Winter

—1962, Trout Pond, NY

Let's take a trip to the outhouse before bed.
These words my grandmother said as though
headed to the five-and-dime or Santa's Workshop
in Upper Jay. As though we'd have pumpkin pie
when we returned to the kitchen to recount our fun.

As if the moon might spill milk on the crust of snow,
and my boots pulled over pajama'd legs would crunch
across the shimmered yard to the odd little shed, its door cut
with magical crescent and sun so both man and woman, boy
and girl could enter there. As though our bottoms

wouldn't settle on the wooden rims of holes, their view
the very bowels of earth, the dank rot of dirt, and that
which exits our bodies and fascinates with visceral smells
exhaled, odors we spend a lifetime denying, our nostrils all
the while perked to aromas of bodily fluids, waste, the scents

of inner workings. As if we wouldn't pretend to ignore
all we evict with a slow creak of the door, the draft
of warmer air within, carried candle lit and placed
on a rough shelf board, as though we wouldn't shut
ourselves away from starlight with the heavy

catalog for browsing, the thinnest pages torn to wipe.
As if we could muzzle the animal in us, cover
our scat with soap and shame, loose from our core
the very iron of blood, black rust of being, the flood
of excrement we shun once we learn to walk upright

as though wholly human. None of this discussed on our trek
back to the house, nor before I turned in for the night,
where carnal breath clung to my pillow and stirred my dreams.

Caged Bird

Much may be made of sorrow, this I know.
My father carved the formless block of wood,
whittling pine to piles of slivered snow.

He believed in trees and bargained they'd see how
to save him from the life of prison guard,
but jailbirds pared his days to slivered snow.

He thought to create, for his daughter, a joyful flow
in the flight of a bird so strangely trapped in wood.
Much may be learned from sorrow, this I know.

He aimed for comfort, yet his knife would show
the rings of sadness underneath the good.
Much will be made of sorrow, this I know.

All those hours he swapped his woodsman's brow—
calm and clear, escaping walled-in moods—
for a life turned into a pile of slivered snow.

He carved out time for winged escape and so
searched for pleasure in a wooden bird.
Much he made of sorrow, this I know,
whittling our precious hours to slivered snow.

Adirondack Girl

*"Adirondacks" is the Algonquin word for "tree-eaters," applied
to the Western Abenaki tribe of New York and Vermont.*

My father's daughter, I roamed the logging trails
behind our house and below the railroad tracks:
one hundred and eighty acres of forest and field.
My father was still a young man. I didn't know

the trails behind our house and below the tracks
fell under the axe of *eminent domain*.
My father, still so young, I couldn't know
how hard a blow it was to lose his land.

Our family fell to the axe of eminent domain.
I used to think my father controlled the world.
How hard a blow it was—to lose our land.
I ran free through stands of oak and birch,

thinking my father must control the world.
I trampled lady's slippers at my feet,
running wild through stands of oak and birch,
and wore a crown of pine needles looped in chains.

I crushed pink lady's slippers at my feet
in a rush to strip the magic bark from pines.
I wore my crown of needles, bound in chains:
a forest trick of nimble-fingered girls.

I rushed to strip the bark from tragic pines
and chewed the needles to a tart green taste.
Forest tricks are for nimble-fingered girls.
My teeth scraped bark to eat what we would lose

soon after I swallowed the needles' tart green taste.
Partridge and pheasant startled, a ruffled flush;
wings skimming bark foretold what we would lose
as my feet parted grass and brush, and I made a wish

(rustled by partridge and pheasant, their startled flush)
that our land would forever and ever remain our land.
Feet parting grass and brush, my heartfelt wish
for my father to hold on tight to his treasured realm.

Our land remains forever our sacred land.
My father's daughter, I roam the logging trails,
the paths I hold so close as my cherished realm:
one hundred and eighty acres of forest and field.

A Prison Guard's Confessions to His Daughter

—1964, Clinton Correctional Facility, Dannemora, NY

Tonight I have to work the wall,
said this man with dread, but more
than saying—his elbows, roosting
birds on a blue, smooth surface
of kitchen table, propped rugged hands
bracing a face of fear and roiling disgrace.
He explained the wall,

its narrow walk, the guard station at each bend,
the intermittent rails. He spoke through fingers thick
with care: *If it weren't for the rails, I couldn't do it.* He wore
a shroud of starched blue shirt and creased gray slacks.
I thought the wooden stick at his waist might keep him safe
from inmate crowds and guards gone sour. *But no,* he said,
the billy club's useless … you see, it's high
and narrow, that concrete wall. There's nothing,
nothing at all to save you if you fall.

He swore that all the cons inside the blocks
could be more or less cajoled into flocks
of obedient, ovine sleep. But the steep
shoulders of sheer wall swelled
like abject fright, capturing him night
after cloistered night. He clutched
the worthless billy club tight, as in his mind
he fell and fell and fell.

When I Tell Her of My Impending Divorce

my grandmother
says to me, *Well*

your grandfather and I never argued
over anything
but cattle.
I wanted them;
he didn't.

This, with a sparkle of tears
underlining dark lashes.

Intussusception

for Florence Elizabeth Bashaw

November, my grandmother warned,
is the saddest month. I try to find this in leaves,
in the cascade of starlings from baring trees, gray
afternoon sky tinged maroon. She, a lover
of lilacs and pansies, rambled barefooted
through pasture, urging rust-patched Jerseys home,
their keening lows a comment on fullness
and need. She mourned the passing

of day before nine, the moon stealing light
before sun has set, whippoorwills and owls
marking its drift across midnight. The eleventh
month carried her to confinement, to darkness
that set the day on edge too soon. The barn cats
curled in the loft, the pony's coat grew long.
Hens, wearied of laying, tucked their beaks
into breast-feathered comforters. Fieldstones cradled
sparks of sun deep in their pits, hunkered down

to meet the cold and snow. My grandmother must have
buried sparks of spring in her waning veins to bear her
forward over the treacherous hump of northern winter.
I wonder, was it the colors of dying, the rusts and browns
of dried blood and excrement, sallow yellows of exudate,
a muted mural of decline that held her hostage, turned ruddy
farm cheeks pallid, quelled the wish to wake again
on that one frosted November dawn when she slipped
through summer and fall, and fell beyond?

My Grandmother in the Hospital for the Last Time

After Jane Kenyon

She is like a soft-eyed Jersey grazing
a stony pasture someone riddles
        with more stones every day
when she's not looking.

        She has ceased to search for the sweetest
grass, and the nourishing stream
        runs shallow. She has lost her bell: we
cannot find her beneath the lowing stars.

        She trips one last time, falls. Someone, please
lead her into the peace of a warm barn,
        help her bed down on clean straw and drift
to her final dream. Someone, please.

My Father's Father, Undone

He knew axes and sawmills,
how to hunt an entire winter
of meals. The way to stoke
a fire so a tiny puff of his
righteous breath and a fisted
page of the Sears catalog
warmed the farmhouse
until tomorrow. How to line
a honeybee hive. With forked
stick, how to find water
snaked beneath soil.
The touchless words to urge
a draft horse to skid logs
in the desired direction.
A good dog.
       But when my grandmother
       died, the homestead shifted.
       He stared at the strange runes
       embedded in her crosswords,
       crumpled in on himself like
       parchment tossed to fire, saltwater
       dissolving the dark resentment
       of her attention to letters.
       He fanned bills across
       the kitchen table
       like a game of canasta
       gone awry, jumbled
       his mounting pile of pills,
       gave away the TV and radio,
       quaked at daily sounds bent
       new and perilous, snapped
       like a rabid badger, suspicious
       of family and old friends.
       Days passed, and the phone

seldom broke the silence
of his final Trout Pond home.
Evenings, a deer rifle balanced
across splayed knees, one palsied
hand covered his eyes. He waited
for whatever would come next
to hunt him.

The Silence of Missing

After Margaret Atwood, "Morning in the Burned House"

In my grandmother's house, I am eating pumpkin pie.
(There is no pie, no house, you understand,
yet I taste the nutmeg and cinnamon, the golden crust.)

My fork chimes against the white, scalloped plate
from five-and-dime china she's owned
forever. I am alone at the table.

Where is my grandfather, my older brother
who sat next to me, eating her pastries
here? A plaid wool work shirt ghosts

a hook by the door and smells of
sawdust. Dishes balance high in the sink
while the tap drips its iron-tainted dirge.

The smudged kitchen window frames
nothing but the shining day
outside its pane, the glint of sun

off long-untended grass, the silence of missing
chickens scratching the driveway dirt.
To the west, a streak of orange and purple

churns late afternoon sky. Light streams in
and lays a slender finger of warning
across the empty Formica expanse.

I don't know if this is sorrow or joy,
finding myself in the house where everything
has vanished, where my grandmother's

sugar bowl and spoon, tea kettle and woodstove
have all gone missing. Where I can't reach out
to hold her welcome hands.

It is the dream I had then, the dream I have now
as I stand here at the window and plunge
my aching arms into soapy water,

dip my plate, scrub and rinse, place it atop
the waiting towel she has spread,
its white cotton a welcome, soothing calm,

my bare child's toes gripping the pine floor,
my flat young chest barely cresting the countertop,
my green eyes burning with her love.

The Shovel

in memory of Florence Elizabeth Bashaw

The shovel leans its curved shadow
along the old barn door, speaks of dying
ways and living memories within the walls
and fences and riverbanks of what was once
my grandmother's farm.

Curious blended smell of machine oil,
metal, rubber, grime: an old tractor has no equal.
A calf in the corner of the kitchen, warm
and silky, her bones drumming hollow thumps
as she nestles into the blanket against
the scarred linoleum floor.

Sunlight glints off red-burnished backs
of roosters while sleek cats arch and purr
at the sight of warm, sweet milk slopped over
the edge of a dented silver pail. The cows,
black-and-white patchwork, neatly lined
in stanchions, chew and think
their harmless cow thoughts.

All this, but most of all, my grandmother's pink calico
apron, dusted with flour and speckled by grease, drapes
itself over her smallish frame and conjures up spicy
pumpkin and smoky fish delights. I can almost
reach and touch her, and see the smiling
crinkles near her eyes, and feel her
thin, strong arms around me
because of that old shovel.

Epitaph for His Draft Horses

After Li-Young Lee

Watch the horses: even while resting
their chests heave and they snort,
working through their equine dreams.

The work is inside you, it is alive
at both ends of your day.
The strain against leather strap

was always welcome, wresting
logs from the trail, harnessing
a great heart to the moment.

Homemade Coffin

Son, build this box of planed and sanded spruce,
though let the boards cure long to store my worth.
Their shade no longer falls across the house,
no stand of wood; new light to air my hearth.
Then lay these limbs in balsam boughs and pine,
add cedar branches. Shortly I must leave
the trees behind, so clothe my body plain—
a flannel shirt and slacks will rightly serve.
The wedding ring I wear does not hold tight
but circles, loose; remove it from my hand—
I need no gold to bind me with its weight.
I'll make my journey, weightless, from this land.

My purpose, unencumbered now by mass,
my spirit, free of gravity at last.

IV.

SNOW MOON

Adirondack Moon

—Upper Jay, NY

From far above Haystack Mountain, you aim your beam
on named stones below, my father's kin

back to the Civil War. One grave moans *Moses*,
whispers that he served. Here under your pallid light

lie my father's father and mother, great-aunt and -uncle,
others whose lineage blurs without first-blood memory

to preserve their worth. In your bluish pall, wild violets
and red clover fade to a slur near the plot where

my father rests. Scattered next to him, my mother's
ashes have sifted underground, rain and gravity

bearing them down, atom by atom, toward
his broken heart. On the other side, his golden

retriever's remains drift their way through soil,
chasing the fading alpha scent.

A finger of your phosphorescence strokes a small
rough stone, leaning alone at the edge of the lot:

    Baby Emily

Who here might have claimed her?
Who is left to ask?

You cast your luster over the simple mark
she made on this world, brief but startling.

How to Swallow

Some days there will be more flowers than the vase can hold.
—Susan Glassmeyer, "I Tell You"
from *The Incomplete Litany of Untold Stories*

A man could not swallow such rich
days. Catching in his throat—
sky and grass, gun and rod, a stallion—

all his to borrow throughout
a miraculous young patch.
How brook trout sprang at his hook,

how this cold bath of dawn slid up
his wading pants as robin and wood thrush
sang to a can of worms and waiting

cast-iron pan, how lilacs hung a fragrant plum
swatch in morning light. How it was a dark risk,
this loving what would pass. Without thinking,

his arms flung broad and willing, vast magic
swarming down so fast—to catch it all was to ask
too much. And too soon, a branch of his body

knowing it couldn't last, a rill cut through air sac
and aorta, warning warp in his path. Almost
drowning but coming up again, a burst of

cognition, a fathoming of hospital cot. How pads
and plastic tubing would rush up in an angry flood,
no wall to hold this back, not a soul looking on

with longing. How in churning narcotic visions,
with mountains of food and drink, and ponds
folding strands of sun from dawn till dusk,

hosting fish as far as a man could cast—his hands
would finally unclasp, his physical form diminish
with a final, lungful waft that would bid us cry

out his awful loss, his past days spat at our morrow, chiding
in that cooling draft: *Don't stop looking, touching,
swallowing—not for an instant, lost!*

Drifting from This World

Imagine the oppressive walls lifting in your lifetime.
The prison bars of tedium peeled away like
the bark of a white birch

canoe bearing you in a bed of pine and balsam between
banks of trillium and pink lady's slippers.
All is light and breath; the sun

is your guide, its warmth holding you over the earth
the way your mother's arms bore you
beside the woodstove,

bathing her new son in firelight and love of home.
Your craft rounds a bend to sunder
an Adirondack stream, and there

trout leap, and a white-tailed doe peers from spruce-cast
shadows, and everywhere you drop your hook
darts a new chance.

Still Life, with Longing

My father asks if I like this
young man who works at a sawmill—his voice urges,

and I think it's the same
as asking if I would like to be an animal instead

of human. Worlds spin between us,
and the boy uses *ain't* in the only sentence he speaks,

a rusty hinge swinging loose
by my ear the rest of the afternoon. He's like Travis

in *Old Yeller*, who wasn't so bad when
I think about it now, now that I'm older and married

to a man who knows little of lumberyards
but loves to read in bed with me every night. And

so Travis, or this lumberyard boy,
is a safe vision of a guileless life, of certain sepia years

we dream while doing our living,
stacking them in a small cedar box, pulling them out

from time to time and breathing
their sweet sawdust scent to the bottom of our lungs.

Call it a world, call it
a quiet patch of forest that's mine. It is nighttime,

my love, and we lie beside
each other, our hands like lovers on the spines

of books, the pages
vague mimes of the pulpwood that gave them birth,

of the trees that couldn't speak
a word of human but nevertheless have borne us toward

more worlds than we could
ever read in a lifetime. The boy-ghost lingers in a corner;

his fingers may have touched
the paper we touch now. His *ain't* may lie inside,

though time has planed
its sharp twang smooth. And my father too

drifts nearby, though among
the trees outside, peering in through my thoughts

to see if everything turned
out the way he meant it. His lips and tongue

no longer form the sounds
we know on Earth, but I hear his voice in my ear,

its timbre low and sure:
Turn out the light, my daughter, before our spirits go.

Canon, Room 346

My older brother gives his last gift to my father,
who is saying goodbye to his children
amid the unearthly drones of hospital marrow.

Aura Lee? he rasps, while my brother culls
random chords from his guitar. But he wants more
than that, our father. He wants every tune he knows

coaxed from strings and wood. Lights dimmed, nurses
listen and whisper behind the door that warns: O_2 in Use.
I don't have time to hear it all, my father might say

had he breath for one more sentence. But instead he gasps out
titles song by song, and we ring his bed like wandering minstrels,
somber tones pooling from the corner where his first son

plays melodies with eyes closed, as if bereft of sight
he could more honestly offer this opus of unchained
love. This night perhaps an otherworld rehearsal, our faces

gathered by sickness, and in health we chant along in slow
and halting phrases, then muster speed and volume as the room
thrums with ancient measures all its own. The monitor

blinks red beats to match my father's last desire, meaning
Weave endless harmony into my unknown journey. He leaves
this world not long after. The last canon of his full attention:

refrains from his children's singing voices, strains of melody
bearing him high above the tedium of dying, into the realm
of redemption, beyond gifts he can no longer rise to claim.

What I Remember Is One Thing

but what my heart remembers
is sunlight shivering on the skin of river,
a field of horses flowing along its banks.
I remember the road dividing
my grandmother's house from ours
and the flagstone walk my father laid,
slab by heavy slab, leading to
our front porch door.

My heart remembers my mother's lap
as she read Br'er Rabbit and Bluebeard
in our postage-stamp front room
and my father's careless whistle rising
from the damp, disheveled cellar where
he repaired the hot-water pipes.

I remember the long climb upstairs
to my bedroom, the closet at the end
of the hall where something perilous
must be hidden, and their voices
rising like shrill gulls in the middle
of night, doors slamming, glass breaking
on the stones of earlier silence.

But my heart remembers my father's
graveled tones blending with distant
thunder as he led us in singing "Old Shep"
before the storm broke. My heart remembers
harmless heat lightning ushering in
a train whistle off to the north,
the hushed chorus of three, huddled
and safe, on their marriage bed.

My Father's Last Night

—March 18, 2006, Champlain Valley Physician's Hospital, NY

He is like an old tractor stalled
on a hillside, red coat fading in the dying
light, shocks of hay left to the night's chill
wind. He no longer pulls the plow back
and forth through the fields, no longer
attaches the blade and cuts a swath
through the deepest grass beside
the river. He remembers the time
the tractor toppled into the water,
steep grade hauling it over, current
snatching him under, he who never
learned to swim. All he could think
to do was not breathe and crawl the river
bottom, a panicked, gill-less creature. Lucky,
with eyes closed tight, he struck out
fast for the nearest bank.

Ferryman, bring me across.
I find no purchase along the riverbed,
and the tractor has finally died.
At last guiltless, I will not hold my breath
as I reach for the other side.

His Last Dog

for Tilly, the best one

He didn't mean to let go of the last
breath he'd ever breathe, of the moon

hung deep in a net of stars, of the mountain's
brow straining to understand

this valley, this shadow. In his hand
a glass trembled, and life canted closer

to its final, breathless hour. He especially
didn't want to miss the last rumble

of Tilly's growling song as her ears tilted
to the squirrel outside the kitchen window.

He didn't want to close his mind to the final soft whine
before steadier hands lifted her from his arms

to a stainless-steel table waiting, her body heavy
with dying. He would have wanted to place

her ashes next to him while dusk crept in
and the sky lost color. He didn't intend to be careless

with the chance to bend where blue gentian,
chicory, and paintbrush burst from the wealth

of her silted bones, to pick a bouquet for the table.
He didn't plan to relinquish so soon

his shared banquet on this marvelous ball, retrieved
by the gentle, ready mouth of the universe.

My Father Has Traveled On

I wonder if he is happier
than he was over here
where we have watermelon
and harmonicas and fiberglass
fishing rods. Does he look back
with nostalgia, remember his first
kiss, think of the way the moon
paddled light across the river
on close summer nights?

He might yearn for ordered days,
plumbing and electricity, his best
horse, that smoothness of harness
under oiled cloth. The smell of sawdust
from the mill, white pine planed to silk.
Certainly there's nothing like root beer
where he rests now. Hours
of pulling weeds——moot in a place
without clutter——and car trouble,
what is that? No talk of taxes or war
in the Middle East, or the ludicrous
cost of butter and milk.

But does he miss the way sunlight slides
across the barn wall all morning and
afternoon, how it is then swallowed
by the rough gray boards, lowered finally
onto the tip of each blade of grass?
Does he yearn for a phrase
to describe that kind of passing,
his mouth empty of words
  ——carburetor, shadows——
in that place over there?

Dear Earth

for Brian, who spread the dog's ashes

When I scattered Tilly across
your rich, loamy breath and she rose

as a shudder of wings into sky
bounding Haystack Mountain,

I was not listening for more
than a whisper of closure

from my father. Goldenrod
nodded approval at cemetery's edge,

turned amber by falling dusk, and he shivered
the depths of empty months underground

where fear of fire interred him
in your arms of worms and minerals

and darkness. No burning desire
stronger than the one to remain

as one's remains. I did not know how
to release him to the air along

with Tilly's ashes, flown to form
the brindled wings of a whippoorwill.

You showed me how the dust
of death becomes a green branch,

how the dog my father cherished
could sing from the outstretched arms

of this unencumbered love,
this loosening grip on ownership.

How I Remember Him

I have climbed the hills of view
        And looked at the world and descended;
I have come by the highway home,
        And lo, it is ended.
                        —Robert Frost, "Reluctance"

Not by the pigeon chest, bowed ribs offering
crippled lungs space to suck in breath,
not the O$_2$ canister riding his side as he pushes
footsteps toward the van, scooter mounted
high inside like an old, mis-stabled steed.
Not the rasp of atmosphere taken in——grim
reminder of two packs a day for forty-plus
unfiltered years——the wheeze of diminished
returns: his careless whistle, missing.

He stands beside his birthright, surveying
Trout Pond, inhaling a clean breeze from above
billowed water, sharp odor of leaves
and turtles and trout sinking fresh and far
into sinless twin bellows, his lure spinning out
to the silver promise of pond burnished by sun,
of white pine and spruce, fish-drenched depths
and sky, swallows and songbirds rowing across
the wind-tillered clouds, all there for the sharing,
unpolluted, inspired into his newest day, pursed
lips unspooling a carefree tune, inflating
his untroubled journey with joy.

Afterword

O. Bashaw and author, 1964

The Ghosts of Horses Who Knew Him

for my father, March 26, 1927–March 18, 2006

They drift to the fence as they graze the pastureland,
though finding the apple in his flat-palmed hand

will be denied. They shuffle forward toward
his disappearance; no jangling bit, no word

to guide them on this shadow trail; no hushed
whistle to harness swiveled ears, lost wish

in the wind. His slowing heart chose spring so
it need not bear the cold of another winter snow:

stark white ground, work stabled out of sight.
In logged clearings they stomp, gather their height

on ponderous hooves, snort wistful dreams and push
aside the long-untended grass and brush,

smelling, tasting for some familiar presence
that will forgive this new, disturbing absence.

The Bashaw Family

Family names and identification, in the order they appear in text and epigraphs:

Oril Vernon Bashaw: Author's father and primary subject of this collection
Carol Bashaw: Oril Bashaw's sister
Moses Bashaw: Oril Bashaw's paternal great-grandfather
Sarah (Joy) Bashaw: Moses Bashaw's wife; Oril Bashaw's paternal great-grandmother
Richard Benedict: Oril Bashaw's maternal grandfather
Martha ("Marthy" Moyer) Benedict: Richard Benedict's wife; Oril Bashaw's maternal grandmother
June Benedict: Oril Bashaw's aunt; sister of Florence Elizabeth (Benedict) Bashaw
Frank Bashaw: Oril Bashaw's paternal grandfather; son of Moses Bashaw
Nellie (Colby) Bashaw: Oril Bashaw's paternal grandmother
Roy Syrill Bashaw: Oril Bashaw's father
William Joy: Oril Bashaw's great-great-uncle; Sarah Joy Bashaw's brother
Rollie Bashaw: Oril Bashaw's paternal great-uncle
Toby Reese Bashaw: Author's older brother; Oril Bashaw's son
Florence Elizabeth (Benedict) Bashaw: Oril Bashaw's mother; wife of Roy Syrill Bashaw
Brian David Bashaw: Author's younger brother; Oril Bashaw's son

*In all instances in the book where I have written "my grandmother" or "my grandfather," I refer to the paternal side of my family.

*Unless otherwise obvious or stated, all italics within the body of poems represent my father's voice in quotation from his unpublished memoir, *See the Moon, Lookum Lots*.

Notes

1. "Sweet Sin, 1939," page 23: According to my father's memoir, the horse collar was often reversed for use on oxen.

2. "The AuSable," page 43: The AuSable River in northeastern New York experiences frequent late winter ice jams and early spring melting and flooding. According to my childhood memories and my parents' stories, many buildings were destroyed either by the large blocks of ice rising out of the river and onto the banks, or by the subsequent flooding washing those banks away. My grandparents' farm, located along the river near Clintonville, NY, lost land along the riverbank nearly every year. The Jehovah's Witnesses Kingdom Hall just down the road from my grandparents' farm was washed away twice in my father's lifetime.

3. "The Tindale Place," page 49: What became my paternal grandparents' farm just outside of Clintonville, NY, was at one time the home of John Tindale from Durham, England. He moved first to Canada and then to upstate New York to engage in the local iron ore mining industry. He married Mary Bowman from Vermont, and John Tindale remained in the house that became known as the "Tindale Place" until his death in 1854. Clintonville for a time became the site of the world's largest bloomer forge, owned by the Peru Steel and Iron Company. The tiny village's population swelled to over thirty thousand during its mining era. When I was a teenager, Clintonville's population vacillated in the range of two hundred to three hundred according to my parents. By 1990, sixteen years before my father died, the population had diminished to ninety-seven residents (U.S. Census data).

4. "The Telling," page 52: A "tell" in a game of poker is a noticeable change in a player's demeanor, giving clues to that player's evaluation of his hand.

5. "Nothing Accidental in the Felling of a Tree," page 54:
The parts of an axe defined:
    Bit: blade
    Head: part extending from bit edge to bit edge (or bit edge to butt in
        a single-bit axe)

Cheeks: smooth sides of axe head
Toe: top corner of the bit
Heel: bottom corner of the bit
Haft: handle
Eye: the hole where the haft is mounted
Shoulder: where the head mounts onto the haft
Belly: longest part of the haft that bows gently
Beard: the part of the bit that extends below the main axe head
Throat: where the haft curves sharply down to the blade assembly of
the axe

6. "A Prison Guard's Confession to His Daughter," page 65: Clinton Correctional Facility in Dannemora, New York's largest and oldest maximum-security institution, was originally a mining prison. In June of 1845, the first fifty prisoners from downstate arrived in shackles, ankle-chains, and striped uniforms after walking the seventeen miles from Plattsburgh, NY. Called "Little Siberia" by many during the years my father worked there as a corrections officer and finally as a sergeant, the prison has housed such well-known inmates as Charles "Lucky" Luciano, Gregory Corso (an original Beat Generation poet), David Berkowitz (Son of Sam), Robert Chambers (the Preppie Killer), Tupac Shakur, and many more.

7. "Intussusception," page 67: The meaning of this word is *a taking within, a telescoping of two parts*. It is also a medical disorder in which a part of the intestine slips inside itself and creates a life-threatening blockage.

8. "How to Swallow," page 80: This poem is a lipogram, meaning that a word or letter usually considered essential has been cut from it. In this case, the title and body of the poem do not contain the letter "e."

C. Ann Kodra grew up in the Adirondack Mountains of New York. She now lives in Knoxville, Tennessee, with her husband. Her poetry and short stories have appeared or are pending in journals and anthologies, including *Birmingham Arts Journal, Blueline, Cavalier Literary Couture, Common Ground Review, Cutthroat* (online), *drafthorse*, MOTIF (vol. 1 & 3), *Now & Then, Peacock Journal, Prime Mincer, Red Truck Review, RHINO, Roanoke Review, Still Crazy, Still: The Journal, The Medulla Review, The Saranac Review, Yemassee,* and others. She is a contributing editor for *New Millennium Writings* and an associate editor for MSI Press.